VINTAGE JESUS

JESUS

TIMELESS ANSWERS *to* TIMELY QUESTIONS

MARK DRISCOLL

THE HUB

1st Edition Published 2008,
2nd Edition Published 2009
3rd Edition Published 2011
by

3405 Milton Avenue, Suite 207
Dallas, TX 75205

Printed in the United States

BIBLE STUDIES

ECCLESIASTES

A Life Well Lived (A Study of Ecclesiastes)
Bible Study Series by Tommy Nelson
> 4 DVD Curriculum
> Companion Study Guide
> A Life Well Lived paperback book

LOVELIFE

NEW! Song of Solomon
Bible Study Series by Mark Driscoll
> 4 DVD Curriculum
> Companion Study Guide
> Packages and bulk discounts available

PHILIPPIANS

NEW! Philippians, To Live is Christ & to Die is Gain
Bible Study Series by Matt Chandler
> 4 DVD Curriculum
> Companion Study Guide
> Packages and bulk discounts available

ROMANS

NEW! Romans, The Letter that Changed the World, Vol. I and II
Bible Study Series by Tommy Nelson
> DVD Curriculum
> Companion Study Guide
> Packages and bulk discounts available

RUTH

NEW! Ruth; Your God, My God. A True Story of Love & Redemption
Bible Study Series by Tommy Nelson
> 4 DVD Curriculum
> Companion Study Guide
> Packages and bulk discounts available

SONG OF SOLOMON

NEW and Improved! 1995 Song of Solomon Classic
DVD Curriculum by Tommy Nelson
> Enhanced video, audio and color graphics
> Updated and enlarged companion Study Guide
> Formatted for Widescreen

NEW! Enhanced SOS for Students
DVD Curriculum by Tommy Nelson
> Re-Mastered Video & Audio
> All new graphics and menus
> Never before seen Q & A's
> All in one Study Guide for both Students & Leaders

www.gotothehub.com

ACKNOWLEDGEMENTS

The Hub wishes to thank the following friends, without whose help, this series and study guide would not have been possible:

Mark Driscoll
Entire Preaching & Theology Branch of Mars Hill Church
Studio recording audience and friends at Mars Hill Church
Jason Johnson
Shatrine Krake
Pocket Pak Albums

We wish to express our sincere gratitude to Crossway Publishers for allowing us the use of all graphics, design and title for Vintage Jesus. This DVD series is an adapation of Mark Driscoll's best selling book of the same title which is published by Crossway. Thank you!

ABOUT THE HUB

Thanks for taking a moment to learn more about us. Our organization began in 1995 working with one speaker, Tommy Nelson and one amazing message, The Song of Solomon. It was and is our privilege to help champion God's written Word on Love, Dating, Marriage and Sex based directly on Song of Solomon. It is a book that has been censored for centuries and it has been a total blessing and thrill to see it change my life, and millions of others.

As of August 2009 we have rebranded our organization to reflect the root of our passion and the future of our organization:

To Develop, Find and Share life changing Bible Centric tools that move people forward. We have renamed our organization to The Hub. It is our passion and commitment to be a Hub for unique, challenging and grace filled resources. I hope you will agree after you participate and interact with one of our resources.

God Bless you and know that if you will listen, God's Truth will move you forward in life, no matter where you have been or are currently.

Doug Hudson, *President - The Hub*

TABLE OF CONTENTS

PAGE

Pastor Mark Driscoll founded Mars Hill Church in Seattle in the fall of 1996. The church has grown from a small Bible study to over 10,000 people. He co-founded and is president of the Acts 29 Church Planting Network which has planted over 200 churches. He has authored The Radical Reformission, Death by Love, Religion Saves, Doctrine and many more.

Most of all, Mark and his high school sweetheart, Grace, enjoy raising their three sons and two daughters.

NEW! Philippians
To Live is Christ & to Die is Gain
Video Teaching Series. Buy. Rent. Download.

The story begins in Philippi. Where Paul introduces three individuals that were all enslaved by the kind of things we often choose over the gospel.

- Lydia, the Business Executive
- The Little Slave Girl
- The Hard Working Jailer

Their lives portray dysfunction and emptiness but are totally transformed by the Gospel. True joy and Christ's love begin to live within them, giving them a life of purpose.

In fact, Paul himself was enslaved and then by God's grace and mercy he could pen these popular and profound words:

To live is Christ & to die is gain
I can do all things through Christ who strengthens me

Let's join Matt Chandler, Pastor of The Village Church in Dallas, Texas, as he walks us through Philippians. In this, one of the most intimate of Paul's letters, he paints a beautiful picture of what it is to be a mature Christian.

About

MATT CHANDLER serves as Lead Pastor of The Village Church in Highland Village, TX. He describes his tenure at The Village as a re-planting effort where he was involved in changing the theological and philosophical culture of the congregation. The church has witnessed a tremendous response growing from 160 people to over 8,000 including satellite campuses in Dallas and Denton. He is one of the most downloaded teachers on iTunes and consistently remains in the Top 5 of all national Religion and Spirituality Podcasts. Matt's passion is to speak to people in America and abroad about the glory of God and beauty of Jesus.

His greatest joy outside of Jesus is being married to Lauren and being a dad to their three children, Audrey, Reid and Norah.

www.gotothehub.com

BEFORE YOU GO ANY FURTHER...READ THIS!

If you are a small group leader, thanks for taking the opportunity to shepherd others along the way. And if you are using this series for personal study, get ready for a life-changing experience you will want to share with others! Here are a few tips as you get started with the series:

- This study was designed with small groups in mind. So put a small group together and get started.
- The series is also perfect for individuals or couples who are looking for ways to deepen their devotions or find practical ways to apply the timeless truths of Scripture.
- This curriculum is designed to be used as either a 12-week or a 6-week study. Each DVD session is 30 minutes long. The sessions are designed to be used as follows: watch each session and then discuss the questions in the study guide.
- Depending on the length of your meeting time, you can watch two sessions per meeting to make this curriculum a 6-week series.
- Mark Driscoll introduces and closes each session. You do not want to miss out on his exhortations that accompany each session!

A WORD TO SMALL GROUP LEADERS

There is no separate leader's guide. Leaders are truly just facilitators of the material: there are no right or wrong answers.

Before each session we encourage leaders to:

- Pray – ask the Lord for guidance on how to lead the members in your group. Pray that He will show you ways to stimulate genuine, dynamic and open communication.
- Preview – it will be very beneficial for you to watch the session before you share it with your group. You will notice the key points from each session and you can better facilitate the discussion questions within your group.
- Prepare – a small group will only go as deep and be as transparent as the leader. If a leader or facilitator is not willing to get personal, then the group will float on the surface. Let God speak through your own struggles and weaknesses.

SESSION ONE

IS JESUS THE ONLY GOD?

Mark 14:61-62

Again the high priest asked him, "Are you the Christ, the Son of the Blessed?" And Jesus said, "I am..."

This question has divided nations, incited political outrage and spawned centuries of theological debate and discourse. No question in life bears upon itself the weight of significance and responsibility that this one does. There are many questions that we can wrongly answer with varying degrees of consequences, but none is more important than this:

Is Jesus the only God?

There are a wide array of views concerning who the person of Jesus was in history and who He is today. Some say He was simply a great teacher, others say a prophet, while others suggest that He was merely a moral man who lived His life well, a worthy example of how we should in turn live our lives.

While there are many views about who Jesus is, what role He played in history and what role He still plays today, no view is more important than the view that Jesus had of Himself. His claims of being one with God the Father, having the power to perform miracles and forgive sin, living in a sinless state of perfection, sitting as the supreme authority over all creation and existing as God in eternity past all demand a response on our part. Will we believe that He is who He claims to be? Or will we consider Him to be a lunatic who died a brutal death on the Cross for His commitment to a series of claims that were ultimately untrue?

In this session we will explore the different historical, social and religious views of who Jesus is, as well as examine some of the claims that Jesus made of Himself as recorded in Scripture. We will then ask the question in response, ***If Jesus is who He says He is, what difference does that make in my life?***

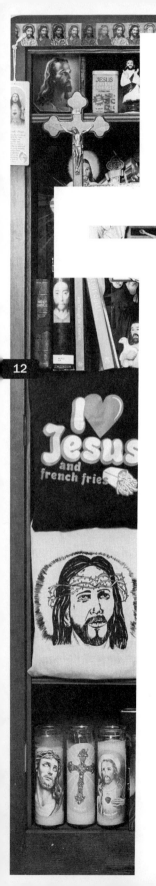

John 6:38
For I have come down from heaven, not to do my own will but the will of him who sent me.

John 10:32
Jesus answered them, "I have shown you many good works from the Father; for which of them are you going to stone me?"

John 8:46
Which one of you convicts me of sin? If I tell the truth, why do you not believe me?

Psalm 51:4
Against you, you only, have I sinned and done what is evil in your sight, so that you may be justified in your words and blameless in your judgment.

Luke 5:20 - 21
And when he saw their faith, he said, "Man, your sins are forgiven you." 21 And the scribes and the Pharisees began to question, saying, "Who is this who speaks blasphemies? Who can forgive sins but God alone?"

Mark 14:61b - 64
Again the high priest asked him, "Are you the Christ, the Son of the Blessed?" 62 And Jesus said, "I am, and you will see the Son of Man seated at the right hand of Power, and coming with the clouds of heaven." 63 And the high priest tore his garments and said, "What further witnesses do we need? 64 You have heard his blasphemy..."

John 8:58 - 59
Jesus said to them, "Truly, truly, I say to you, before Abraham was, I am." 59 So they picked up stones to throw at him, but Jesus hid himself and went out of the temple.

John 10:30 - 33
I and the Father are one." 31 The Jews picked up stones again to stone him. 32 Jesus answered them, "I have shown you many good works from the Father; for which of them are you going to stone me?" 33 The Jews answered him, "It is not for a good work that

we are going to stone you but for blasphemy, because you, being a man, make yourself God."

Deuteronomy 6:4
Hear, O Israel: The LORD our God, the LORD is one.

Matthew 28:18
And Jesus came and said to them, "All authority in heaven and on earth has been given to me.

John 14:6
Jesus said to him, "I am the way, and the truth, and the life. No one comes to the Father except through me.

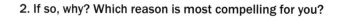

DISCUSSION QUESTIONS

1. Do you believe that Jesus is the only God?

_____

_____

_____

> *There are a ton of questions that you can get wrong throughout life with varying degrees of pain and difficulty. This question, however, is the most important.*

14

2. If so, why? Which reason is most compelling for you?

_____

_____

_____

3. In your opinion, why do people struggle to believe the claims that Jesus made about Himself?

_____

_____

_____

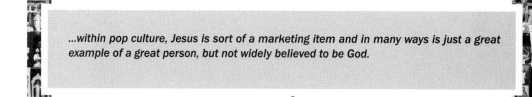

> *...within pop culture, Jesus is sort of a marketing item and in many ways is just a great example of a great person, but not widely believed to be God.*

4. How do you see Jesus viewed in popular culture today?

_____

_____

_____

> ...Jesus clearly, emphatically, repeatedly said, "I am God."

5. Who do you need to speak with about Jesus, answering any questions he or she may have about Him?

_____

_____

_____

15

KEY THOUGHT

Everything hinges on whether or not you believe Jesus is God, including the quality of life that you live today and the eternity of life that you'll have after this life.

PRAYER REQUESTS

_____

_____

_____

_____

_____

NOTES

_____

_____

_____

_____

_____

_____

HOW HUMAN WAS JESUS?

John 1:14

And the Word became flesh and dwelt among us...

Jesus lived life as an ordinary man from an ordinary town. He was born into humble circumstances and died a humiliating death. He knew a full range of human emotions. He wept at the loss of a friend and rejoiced over the ministry of His disciples. He showed compassion to a group of hungry people and got angry at a bunch of swindlers. He became intensely frustrated with the religious elite and He deeply loved His closest disciples.

Jesus also knew, in a deep and profound way, the full range of physical suffering. From hunger pains to growing pains, Jesus was well acquainted with the daily physical needs of the human body. And upon His brutal death, He suffered the most severe of all pain—the sting of sin poured out upon His back.

While Jesus subjected Himself to nothing less than full humanity, He never once compromised the fullness of His divinity. He was at all times fully God and fully man. Jesus lived and breathed as a man yet never once ceased to be that which He had always been – the omniscient, omnipotent, supremely perfect God of the universe.

To know and follow the true Jesus, we must understand Him as both fully God and fully man. To set aside His divinity and overemphasize His humanity is to turn Him into nothing more than a great moral teacher with no real power or authority. To disregard His humanity and focus exclusively on His divinity is to turn Him into an inaccessible, distant God that cannot fully relate to the condition of fallen humanity.

In this session we will explore how human Jesus really was. We will also address a host of issues that arise around this subject, questions such as, "If Jesus was fully man then was He something less than God?" and "If Jesus was fully God, how could He truly have been tempted as a man?"

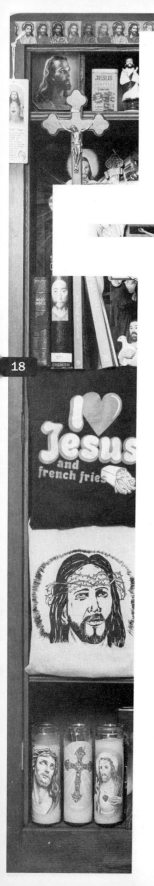

Isaiah 53:2

For he grew up before him like a young plant, and like a root out of dry ground; he had no form or majesty that we should look at him, and no beauty that we should desire him.

Luke 2:52

And Jesus increased in wisdom and in stature and in favor with God and man.

1 Timothy 2:5

For there is one God, and there is one mediator between God and men, the man Christ Jesus,

Matthew 1:18 - 25

Now the birth of Jesus Christ took place in this way. When his mother Mary had been betrothed to Joseph, before they came together she was found to be with child from the Holy Spirit. 19 And her husband Joseph, being a just man and unwilling to put her to shame, resolved to divorce her quietly. 20 But as he considered these things, behold, an angel of the Lord appeared to him in a dream, saying, "Joseph, son of David, do not fear to take Mary as your wife, for that which is conceived in her is from the Holy Spirit. 21 She will bear a son, and you shall call his name Jesus, for he will save his people from their sins." 22 All this took place to fulfill what the Lord had spoken by the prophet: 23 "Behold, the virgin shall conceive and bear a son, and they shall call his name Immanuel"(which means, God with us). 24 When Joseph woke from sleep, he did as the angel of the Lord commanded him: he took his wife, 25 but knew her not until she had given birth to a son. And he called his name Jesus.

John 1:1 - 18

In the beginning was the Word, and the Word was with God, and the Word was God. 2 He was in the beginning with God. 3 All things were made through him, and without him was not any thing made that was made. 4 In him was life, and the life was the light of men. 5 The light shines in the darkness, and the darkness has not overcome it. 6 There was a man sent from God, whose name was John. 7 He came as a witness, to bear witness about the light, that all might believe through him. 8 He was not the light, but came to bear witness about the light. 9 The true light, which enlightens everyone, was coming into the world. 10 He was in the world, and the world was made through him, yet the world did not know him. 11 He came to his own, and his own people did not receive him. 12 But to all who did receive him, who believed in his name, he gave the right to become children of God, 13 who were born, not of blood nor of the will of the flesh nor of the will of man, but of God. 14 And the Word became flesh and dwelt among us, and we have seen his glory, glory as of the only Son from the Father, full of grace and truth. 15 (John bore witness about him, and cried out, "This was he of whom I said, 'He who comes after me ranks before me, because he was before me.'") 16 And from his fullness we have all received, grace upon grace. 17 For the law was given through Moses; grace and truth came through Jesus Christ. 18 No one has ever seen God; the only God, who is at the Father's side, he has made him known.

Philippians 2:5 - 11

Have this mind among yourselves, which is yours in Christ Jesus, 6 who, though he was in the form of God, did not count equality with God a thing to be grasped, 7 but made himself nothing, taking the form of a servant, being born in the likeness of men. 8 And being found in human form, he humbled himself by becoming obedient to the point of death, even death on a cross. 9 Therefore God has highly exalted him and bestowed on him the name that is above every name, 10 so that at the name of Jesus every knee should bow, in heaven and on earth and under the earth, 11 and every tongue confess that Jesus Christ is Lord, to the glory of God the Father.

Hebrews 4:15

For we do not have a high priest who is unable to sympathize with our weaknesses, but one who in every respect has been tempted as we are, yet without sin.

Luke 3:21 - 22

Now when all the people were baptized, and when Jesus also had been baptized and was praying, the heavens were opened, 22 and the Holy Spirit descended on him in bodily form, like a dove; and a voice came from heaven, "You are my beloved Son; with you I am well pleased."

1. What does Jesus' humanity mean for you?

_____

_____

_____

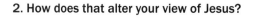

Jesus was not just a numb, emotionless spiritual robot.

20

2. How does that alter your view of Jesus?

_____

_____

_____

3. In what ways does this make Him more accessible for you?

_____

_____

_____

"Christ added to Himself which He was not. He did not lose what He was." ~ Augustine

4. How would you explain the "hypostatic union" to someone?

_____

_____

_____

> *...for those who want to know who God is, they need to look to Jesus because no one will see God apart from Him.*

5. Why is it so important to know that Jesus was fully God and fully man?

_____

_____

_____

KEY THOUGHT

Jesus came as God in flesh, so for those who want to know God, they must first look to Jesus.

PRAYER REQUESTS

_____

_____

_____

_____

_____

NOTES

_____

_____

_____

_____

_____

SESSION THREE

HOW DID PEOPLE KNOW JESUS WAS COMING?

Luke 24:44

"...everything written about me in the Law of Moses and the Prophets and the Psalms must be fulfilled."

Jesus Christ alone is the central theme of Scripture. Through Old Testament prophecy and its perfect New Testament historical and future fulfillment, Jesus is clearly revealed as the Messiah, the great Hero of the epoch story of God. The whole of Scripture then is rightly understood only when the Person and work of Jesus are the central truths being revealed.

The presence of clearly defined and specifically fulfilled prophecy distinguishes Christianity from all other major world religions and establishes the Word of God as fully reliable and authoritative in nature. Although written through the hands of multiple authors over the span of four thousand years, the consistency of Old Testament prophecies about Jesus is flawless, attributable only to the sovereignty of God and the power of His inspired Word.

Jesus boldly proclaimed Himself to be the fulfillment of all Old Testament prophecy. Specifics of His birth, life, death and resurrection were clearly foretold centuries before their actualization. Any serious student of the Old Testament would have known, in no uncertain terms, that Jesus was the One the Old Testament prophecies spoke of. He was God in flesh whose entrance into human history came at the exact time and under the exact circumstances as was prophesied in the Old Testament.

In this session we will examine how God used prophecy to prepare His people for the coming of Jesus the Messiah. We will explore several Old Testament passages along with their corresponding New Testament fulfillments in order to demonstrate clearly the authority of God's Word and His sovereignty over all of time.

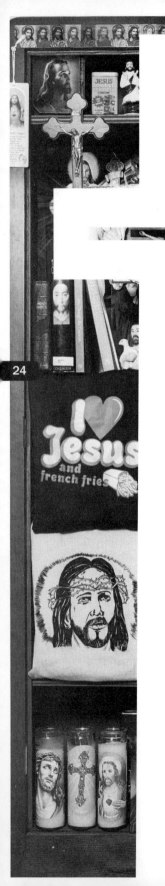

Matthew 5:17

"Do not think that I have come to abolish the Law or the Prophets; I have not come to abolish them but to fulfill them.

John 5:39 - 40

You search the Scriptures because you think that in them you have eternal life; and it is they that bear witness about me, 40 yet you refuse to come to me that you may have life.

Luke 24:44

Then he said to them, "These are my words that I spoke to you while I was still with you, that everything written about me in the Law of Moses and the Prophets and the Psalms must be fulfilled."

Psalm 22:16

For dogs encompass me; a company of evildoers encircles me; they have pierced my hands and feet.—

Isaiah 52:13 – Isaiah 53:12

Behold, my servant shall act wisely; he shall be high and lifted up, and shall be exalted. 14 As many were astonished at you—his appearance was so marred, beyond human semblance, and his form beyond that of the children of mankind— 15 so shall he sprinkle many nations; kings shall shut their mouths because of him; for that which has not been told them they see, and that which they have not heard they understand. 53:1 Who has believed what he has heard from us? And to whom has the arm of the LORD been revealed? 2 For he grew up before him like a young plant, and like a root out of dry ground; he had no form or majesty that we should look at him, and no beauty that we should desire him. 3 He was despised and rejected by men; a man of sorrows, and acquainted with grief; and as one from whom men hide their faces he was despised, and we esteemed him not. 4 Surely he has borne our griefs and carried our sorrows; yet we esteemed him stricken, smitten by God, and afflicted. 5 But he was wounded for our transgressions; he was crushed for our iniquities; upon him was the chastisement that brought us peace, and with his stripes we are healed. 6 All we like sheep have gone astray; we have turned—every one—to his own way; and the LORD has laid on him the iniquity of us all. 7 He was oppressed, and he was afflicted, yet he opened not his mouth; like a lamb that is led to the slaughter, and like a sheep that before its shearers is silent, so he opened not his mouth. 8 By oppression and judgment he was taken away; and as for his generation, who considered that he was cut off out of the land of the living, stricken for the transgression of my people? 9 And they made his grave with the wicked and with a rich man in his death, although he had done no violence, and there was no deceit in his mouth. 10 Yet it was the will of the LORD to crush him; he has put him to grief; when his soul makes an offering for guilt, he shall see his offspring; he shall prolong his days; the will of the LORD shall prosper in his hand. 11 Out of the anguish of his soul he shall see and be satisfied by his knowledge shall the righteous one, my servant, make many to be accounted righteous, and he shall bear their iniquities. 12 Therefore I will divide him a portion with the many, and he shall divide the spoil with the strong, because he poured out his soul to death and was numbered with the transgressors; yet he bore the sin of many, and makes intercession for the transgressors.

Isaiah 35:5 - 6
Then the eyes of the blind shall be opened, and the ears of the deaf unstopped; 6 then shall the lame man leap like a deer, and the tongue of the mute sing for joy. For waters break forth in the wilderness, and streams in the desert;

Micah 5:2
But you, O Bethlehem Ephrathah, who are too little to be among the clans of Judah, from you shall come forth for me one who is to be ruler in Israel, whose coming forth is from of old, from ancient days.

Zechariah 9:9; 11:12 - 13
Rejoice greatly, O daughter of Zion! Shout aloud, O daughter of Jerusalem! Behold, your king is coming to you; righteous and having salvation is he, humble and mounted on a donkey, on a colt, the foal of a donkey. 11:12 - 13 Then I said to them, "If it seems good to you, give me my wages; but if not, keep them." And they weighed out as my wages thirty pieces of silver. 13 Then the LORD said to me, "Throw it to the potter"— the lordly price at which I was priced by them. So I took the thirty pieces of silver and threw them into the house of the LORD, to the potter.

Malachi 3:1
"Behold, I send my messenger, and he will prepare the way before me. And the Lord whom you seek will suddenly come to his temple; and the messenger of the covenant in whom you delight, behold, he is coming, says the LORD of hosts.

DISCUSSION QUESTIONS

1. Which prophecies were most compelling, convincing and convicting for you?

_____
_____
_____
_____

> ...about 25% of the Old Testament was prophetic in nature – meaning it was predicting future events. This shows two things: one, that God is sovereign over human history, and two, that the Bible is true because it is information that people would only know if it was revealed to them about God.

2. In what ways does this make the Bible more reliable and authoritative for you?

_____
_____
_____
_____

3. In what ways does this make Him more accessible for you?

_____
_____
_____
_____

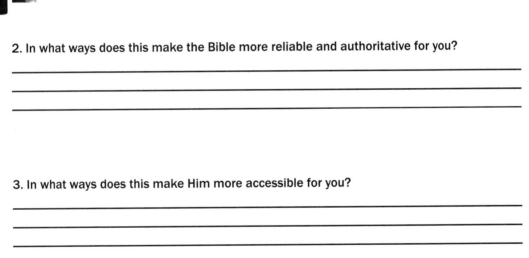

> It's a miracle that people would know in this kind of detail how Jesus would come, live, die and rise.
>
> I have no other way to explain the specificity regarding the anticipation of the coming of Jesus, other than God wrote through people. And He knows history and rules over it in sovereignty.

4. What would your response be to someone who claims that Jesus simply manipulated His life in such a way that He would fulfill all the Old Testament prophecies?

_____

_____

_____

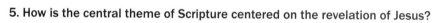

All of the prophetic promises are fulfilled in Jesus.

Here's the bottom line: God rules over history. God wrote the Bible. The Bible and history are all about Jesus.

5. How is the central theme of Scripture centered on the revelation of Jesus?

_____

_____

_____

KEY THOUGHT

The Old Testament was anticipatory and preparatory to the coming of Jesus the Messiah.

PRAYER REQUESTS

NOTES

NOTES

WHY DID JESUS COME TO EARTH?

John 20:21

As the Father has sent me, even so I am sending you.

Jesus came to earth as a missionary. He learned the culture, adapted to the customs, developed relationships with the locals and spoke truth into their circumstances in a way they could understand. His entrance into human history shows us the extent of the love of God and the lengths He is willing to go to rescue and redeem sinners.

Among the many roles Jesus played, Scripture most consistently identifies Him as holding the offices of prophet, priest and king.

The prophets of the Old Testament were truth-tellers. They spoke the word of God with authority, conviction and urgency. They were commissioned by God and granted all authority to speak on His behalf. Because of the boldness and severity of their call on peoples and nations to repent of their sins and turn to God, they were often threatened, hated, persecuted and killed. Like the Old Testament prophets, Jesus came with the authority of God to proclaim, declare and preach the truth of the gospel with conviction and boldness.

The role of the priest in the Old Testament was to act as a middle-man or mediator between God and man. The priests loved the people, showed them compassion and encouraged them in their times of need. They taught the word of God and instructed people in the way they should live. They also took upon themselves the sins of the people and confessed them to God on their behalf. Like the Old Testament priests, Jesus came as our great High Priest, the Mediator between God and man. He showed us compassion, grace and mercy and took our sins upon Himself so that we might be in right relationship with God.

The kings of the Old Testament were honored and revered. They ruled with power, dominion and authority over great and mighty kingdoms. They were set apart and respected as ones who were worthy of honor and praise, adoration and obedience. Jesus as King is currently ruling over all powers, authorities, dominions and offices of the physical and spiritual world. He rules over all nations, political movements, social agendas and religious dispositions. He sits on the throne, high and lifted up, and reigns supreme as the One who is worthy of all honor and glory and praise.

In this session we will explore how Jesus is perfectly prophet, priest and king and discuss why it is critically important for us to know Him in the fullness of this capacity in our lives.

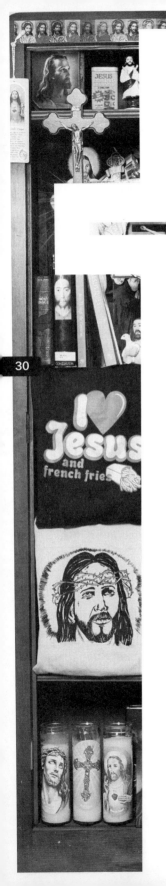

John 20:21

As the Father has sent me, even so I am sending you.

Matthew 5:22

But I say to you... that everyone who is angry with his brother shall be guilty before the court; and whoever says to his brother, 'You good-for-nothing,' shall be guilty before the supreme court; and whoever says, 'You fool,' shall be guilty enough to go into the fiery hell.

Matthew 5:28

But I say to you...that everyone who looks at a woman with lust for her has already committed adultery with her in his heart.

Matthew 5:32

But I say to you... that everyone who divorces his wife, except for the reason of unchastity, makes her commit adultery; and whoever marries a divorced woman commits adultery.

Matthew 5:34

But I say to you... make no oath at all, either by heaven, for it is the throne of God.

Matthew 5:39

But I say to you... do not resist an evil person; but whoever slaps you on your right cheek, turn the other to him also.

Matthew 5:44

But I say to you... love your enemies and pray for those who persecute you.

Hebrews 4:15 - 16

For we do not have a high priest who is unable to sympathize with our weaknesses, but one who in every respect has been tempted as we are, yet without sin. 16 Let us then with confidence draw near to the throne of grace, that we may receive mercy and find grace to help in time of need.

2 Samuel 7:12 - 13

When your days are fulfilled and you lie down with your fathers, I will raise up your offspring after you, who shall come from your body, and I will establish his kingdom. 13 He shall build a house for my name, and I will establish the throne of his kingdom forever.

DISCUSSION QUESTIONS

1. Do you most easily identify with Jesus as prophet, priest or king?

_____

_____

_____

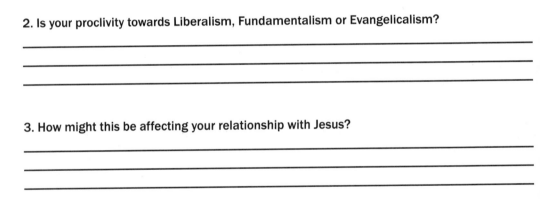

Traditional Christian theology has always held that Jesus occupies these three offices of prophet, priest and king. And that He does so in fulfillment of the Old Testament expectations.

2. Is your proclivity towards Liberalism, Fundamentalism or Evangelicalism?

_____

_____

_____

3. How might this be affecting your relationship with Jesus?

_____

_____

_____

... Jesus coming into history shows us the love of God and the lengths that God is willing to go to accommodate us.

The Old Testament prophets would appeal to God for their authority. Jesus appealed to Himself as God for His authority.

4. How has your life been affected by someone who failed to present to you the full picture of who Jesus is?

_____

_____

_____

> *Jesus is prophet. Jesus is priest. Jesus is king. He comes as a missionary into human history to serve us in these various ways...*

5. What steps can you take to develop a fuller, more complete understanding of the person and work of Jesus?

_____

_____

_____

KEY THOUGHT

Jesus is prophet. Jesus is priest. Jesus is king. He comes as a missionary into human history to serve us in these various ways.

PRAYER REQUESTS

_____

_____

_____

_____

_____

NOTES

_____

_____

_____

_____

_____

_____

NOTES

34

WHY DID JESUS' MOM NEED TO BE A VIRGIN?

Isaiah 7:14

Therefore the Lord himself will give you a sign. Behold, the virgin shall conceive and bear a son, and shall call his name Immanuel.

Some call it myth, some call it folklore and some celebrate it as truth every year at Christmas. Outside of His resurrection from the grave, Jesus' miraculous birth through the womb of a young virgin is historically one of the most controversial tenants of the Christian belief system. Opinions about the virgin birth of Jesus to His young, unwed mother Mary vary greatly, but Scripture speaks clearly about the matter even in its opening pages.

In Genesis, some 4,000 years before Jesus arrived on the scene, God was already preparing people for His coming. In Isaiah, nearly 700 years before the birth of Jesus, the prophet was declaring the coming of the Messiah and the circumstances of His virgin birth. And in the Gospels, just before Jesus' birth, the angels visit His young parents-to-be and inform them that God has chosen them to be mother and father to the Savior of the world. Scared, confused and probably a bit overwhelmed, the young virgin Mary humbly accepts the role, and her young fiancé, Joseph, stays by her side.

The birth of Jesus through the virgin Mary took place to fulfill the Old Testament promises, and to point to Him yet again as the One whom all of history had been anticipating. Belief in the virgin birth of Jesus is essential for all serious studiers of the Bible and followers of Jesus. It not only validates the authority of Scripture, but it also provides a clear and compelling call on our lives to live with the type of faith that characterized the young virgin Mary.

Scripture never calls us to worship Mary, pray to her or pay homage to her as a deified human. She was a simple girl who God used to accomplish arguably one of the most profound miracles in human history. Mary is not to be our object of faith, but she is an incredible example of faith. Her life of character, faith and virtue are certainly worth modeling.

In this session we will explore what the Bible has to say about the birth of Jesus and discover why a young, unwed virgin named Mary had to be His mom.

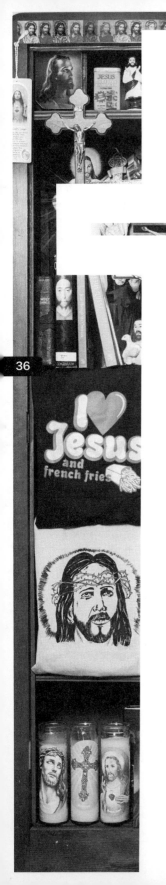

Genesis 3:15

I will put enmity between you and the woman, and between your offspring and her offspring; he shall bruise your head, and you shall bruise his heel."

Isaiah 7:14

Therefore the Lord himself will give you a sign. Behold, the virgin shall conceive and bear a son, and shall call his name Immanuel.

Matthew 1:18 - 25

Now the birth of Jesus Christ took place in this way. When his mother Mary had been betrothed to Joseph, before they came together she was found to be with child from the Holy Spirit. 19 And her husband Joseph, being a just man and unwilling to put her to shame, resolved to divorce her quietly. 20 But as he considered these things, behold, an angel of the Lord appeared to him in a dream, saying, "Joseph, son of David, do not fear to take Mary as your wife, for that which is conceived in her is from the Holy Spirit. 21 She will bear a son, and you shall call his name Jesus, for he will save his people from their sins." 22 All this took place to fulfill what the Lord had spoken by the prophet: 23 "Behold, the virgin shall conceive and bear a son, and they shall call his name Immanuel" (which means, God with us). 24 When Joseph woke from sleep, he did as the angel of the Lord commanded him: he took his wife, 25 but knew her not until she had given birth to a son. And he called his name Jesus.

Luke 2:1 - 21

In those days a decree went out from Caesar Augustus that all the world should be registered. 2 This was the first registration when Quirinius was governor of Syria. 3 And all went to be registered, each to his own town. 4 And Joseph also went up from Galilee, from the town of Nazareth, to Judea, to the city of David, which is called Bethlehem, because he was of the house and lineage of David, 5 to be registered with Mary, his betrothed, who was with child. 6 And while they were there, the time came for her to give birth. 7 And she gave birth to her firstborn son and wrapped him in swaddling cloths and laid him in a manger, because there was no place for them in the inn. The Shepherds and the Angels. 8 And in the same region there were shepherds out in the field, keeping watch over their flock by night. 9 And an angel of the Lord appeared to them, and the glory of the Lord shone around them, and they were filled with fear. 10 And the angel said to them, "Fear not, for behold, I bring you good news of great joy that will be for all the people. 11 For unto you is born this day in the city of David a Savior, who is Christ the Lord. 12 And this will be a sign for you: you will find a baby wrapped in swaddling cloths and lying in a manger." 13 And suddenly there was with the angel a multitude of the heavenly host praising God and saying, 14 "Glory to God in the highest, and on earth peace among those with whom he is pleased!" 15 When the angels went away from them into heaven, the shepherds said to one another, "Let us go over to Bethlehem and see this thing that has happened, which the Lord has made known to us." 16 And they went with haste and found Mary and Joseph, and the baby lying in a manger. 17 And when they saw it, they made known the saying that had been told them concerning this child. 18 And all who heard it wondered at what the shepherds told them. 19 But Mary treasured up all these things, pondering them in her heart. 20 And the shepherds returned, glorifying and praising God for all they had heard and seen, as it had been told them. 21 And at the end of eight days, when he was circumcised, he was called Jesus, the name given by the angel before he was conceived in the womb.

DISCUSSION QUESTIONS

1. [Just for Men] What can you learn from the example of Joseph?

_____
_____
_____

> *"I would like to ask Him (Jesus) if He was indeed virgin born. The answer to that question would define history for me."* ~ Larry King

2. [Just for Women] What can you learn from the example of Mary?

_____
_____
_____

3. What does Scripture NOT teach about the virgin Mary?

_____
_____
_____

> ...that's what sinners need. We need a Savior. We need somebody to help us. We need somebody to come get us. We need somebody to come along beside us, and that is Jesus.

> I believe everything that the Scriptures say about the virgin birth of Jesus is true. But lots of churches, denominations, traditions and theologians have added all kinds of false teaching or at least erroneous teaching.

4. Why is it important to believe that Jesus was born of the virgin Mary?

_____

_____

_____

> *Here's what I think is so important about Mary...Catholics have made too much of her. Protestants have made too little of her...The truth is that she should be lauded as an example of great faith.*

5. How would you answer someone who claims the idea that Jesus was virgin born is simply a myth?

_____

_____

KEY THOUGHT

The virgin birth of Jesus was one of the ways that God made it clear that Jesus is the One that all of history was anticipating.

PRAYER REQUESTS

_____

_____

_____

_____

_____

NOTES

_____

_____

_____

_____

_____

NOTES

40

SESSION SIX

WHAT DID JESUS ACCOMPLISH ON THE CROSS?

2 Corinthians 5:21

For our sake he made him to be sin who knew no sin, so that in him we might become the righteousness of God.

The cross has become the most recognizable symbol in all of history. We wear them around our necks, hang them on our living room walls and attach them to the top of our church buildings. All of this is quite astonishing considering its brutal and violent history as a means of torture and horrific capital punishment. And perhaps it is this nonchalant attitude towards the cross that has left so many unable to fully grasp the severity of Christ's crucifixion and the magnitude of His sacrifice.

But why did Jesus have to go to the Cross and what did His brutal death there accomplish?

The Bible repeatedly uses the little word *for* to explain how the heinous and disgusting murder of Jesus could actually be called Good News and celebrated as such every Good Friday. This one little word carries much theological significance, explaining how Jesus paid the penalty for our sins by dying in our place for our sins so that we could be in right relationship with God.

Through the Cross we see the love and the wrath of God on display together in a profound way. His perfect love for us was demonstrated through His perfect wrath being poured out upon His Son. And through it all, Jesus said very little but accomplished much. The blood He shed as the perfect Lamb was sufficient for our sins. His sacrifice was final.

Jesus accomplished on the Cross what sinful man could not have accomplished on his own. He took our sin and exchanged it for His righteousness. He took our shame and exchanged it for His glory. He took our death and exchanged it for His life. It is only through His grace that we can stand justified before God. This indeed is good news.

In this session we will explore in detail the historical event of Jesus' crucifixion and discuss the theological implications behind what it accomplished.

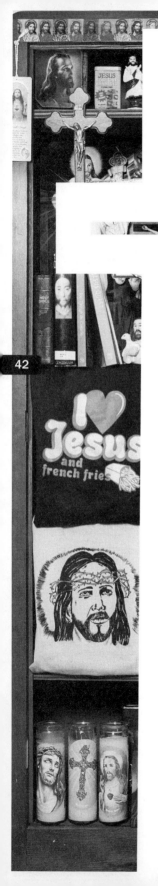

Deuteronomy 21:22 - 23

"And if a man has committed a crime punishable by death and he is put to death, and you hang him on a tree, 23 his body shall not remain all night on the tree, but you shall bury him the same day, for a hanged man is cursed by God. You shall not defile your land that the LORD your God is giving you for an inheritance.

Luke 23:34a

Father, forgive them...

Isaiah 53:5

But he was wounded for our transgressions; he was crushed for our iniquities; upon him was the chastisement that brought us peace, and with his stripes we are healed.

Isaiah 53:12

Therefore I will divide him a portion with the many, and he shall divide the spoil with the strong, because he poured out his soul to death and was numbered with the transgressors; yet he bore the sin of many, and makes intercession for the transgressors.

Romans 4:25

...who was delivered up for our trespasses and raised for our justification.

Romans 5:8

...but God shows his love for us in that while we were still sinners, Christ died for us.

1 Corinthians 15:3

For I delivered to you as of first importance what I also received: that Christ died for our sins in accordance with the Scriptures...

1 Peter 3:18

For Christ also suffered once for sins, the righteous for the unrighteous, that he might bring us to God, being put to death in the flesh but made alive in the spirit...

1 John 2:2

He is the propitiation for our sins, and not for ours only but also for the sins of the whole world.

Galatians 3:13

Christ redeemed us from the curse of the law by becoming a curse for us—for it is written, "Cursed is everyone who is hanged on a tree"...

2 Corinthians 5:21

For our sake he made him to be sin who knew no sin, so that in him we might become the righteousness of God.

1 John 4:10

And this is love, not that we have loved God, but that God has loved us, and He sent Jesus to be the propitiation, the substitute, for our sins.

John 1:29

Behold, the Lamb of God who takes away the sins of the world.

THE CHRISTOLOGY OF JESUS

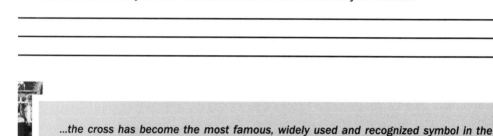

DISCUSSION QUESTIONS

1. What sin issues in your life did Jesus take to the Cross on your behalf?

_____

_____

_____

> *...the cross has become the most famous, widely used and recognized symbol in the history of the world...*

2. What does the crucifixion of Jesus say about how seriously God takes sin?

_____

_____

_____

3. How are the perfect love and perfect wrath of God both put on display through the Cross?

_____

_____

_____

> *Part of my concern is that Christians become so familiar with the cross of Jesus that we treat it almost like a marketing slogan or a concept that we quickly pass through – "Jesus died for all your sins," which is absolutely true, but it's imperative that we slow down and understand crucifixion in its historical context.*

> *Jesus saw all who hated and despised Him and in great love and affection Jesus said, in His moment of great torment, "Father, forgive them."*

4. How did the Old Testament sacrificial system anticipate and foreshadow the coming of Jesus?

_____

_____

_____

> *God is loving and wrathful. And on the cross we see both God's love and wrath working together perfectly.*

5. Who in your life needs to hear about the severity and the beauty of Jesus' death on the Cross?

_____

_____

_____

KEY THOUGHT

Jesus paid our penalty for sin by dying in our place for our sin, so that we could be one with God.

PRAYER REQUESTS

_____

_____

_____

_____

_____

NOTES

_____

_____

_____

_____

_____

NOTES

DID JESUS RISE FROM DEATH?

1 Corinthians 15:4
...he was raised on the third day in accordance with the Scriptures...

The Apostle Paul says that if Jesus did not rise from the dead, then the entire Christian faith is built on myth and as a result, is worthless. Therefore, the question of whether or not Jesus rose from death is absolutely essential to what it means to be a Christian. Without His physical, bodily resurrection, Jesus' claims of divinity and eternality are null and void, and His promise of eternal life to those who would trust Him is blasphemous. All of the Christian faith hinges upon this essential truth – Jesus died on the Cross, was buried and on the third day rose from death.

The resurrection of Jesus is supported by both biblically and historically verifiable pieces of evidence. Biblically, some 700 years prior to His birth, the prophet Isaiah speaks of Jesus' rising from the grave. Even Jesus Himself speaks openly about His death and subsequent resurrection from the dead. Historically, there was eyewitness testimony from hundreds who saw the nail-scarred hands and feet of the resurrected Jesus. As well, the social, political and religious transformation that occurred through this one man's life, death and resurrection is unparalleled in all of history.

While many object to the biblical and historical account of the resurrection of Jesus, their arguments fail to satisfy the burden of proof sufficiently. They are simply meager attempts to skirt out from underneath the implications of Jesus' resurrection in their own lives.

In this session we will discuss the doctrine of the resurrection of Jesus from death and explore why Christians believe that Jesus, unlike any other man in history, returned from death fully, totally and completely alive.

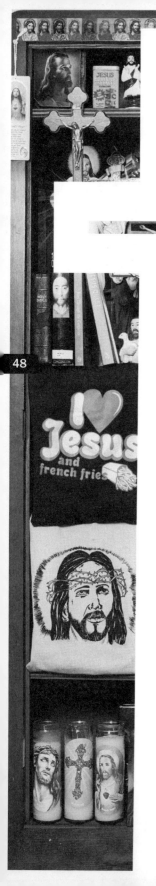

Isaiah 53:8 - 11

By oppression and judgment he was taken away; and as for his generation, who considered that he was cut off out of the land of the living, stricken for the transgression of my people? 9 And they made his grave with the wicked and with a rich man in his death, although he had done no violence, and there was no deceit in his mouth. 10 Yet it was the will of the LORD to crush him; he has put him to grief; when his soul makes an offering for guilt, he shall see his offspring; he shall prolong his days; the will of the LORD shall prosper in his hand. 11 Out of the anguish of his soul he shall see and be satisfied; by his knowledge shall the righteous one, my servant, make many to be accounted righteous, and he shall bear their iniquities.

Mark 8:31

And he began to teach them that the Son of Man must suffer many things and be rejected by the elders and the chief priests and the scribes and be killed, and after three days rise again.

Mark 9:30 - 31

They went on from there and passed through Galilee. And he did not want anyone to know, 31 for he was teaching his disciples, saying to them, "The Son of Man is going to be delivered into the hands of men, and they will kill him. And when he is killed, after three days he will rise."

Mark 10:33 - 34

...saying, "See, we are going up to Jerusalem, and the Son of Man will be delivered over to the chief priests and the scribes, and they will condemn him to death and deliver him over to the Gentiles. 34 And they will mock him and spit on him, and flog him and kill him. And after three days he will rise."

Luke 24:1 - 36

But on the first day of the week, at early dawn, they went to the tomb, taking the spices they had prepared. 2 And they found the stone rolled away from the tomb, 3 but when they went in they did not find the body of the Lord Jesus. 4 While they were perplexed about this, behold, two men stood by them in dazzling apparel. 5 And as they were frightened and bowed their faces to the ground, the men said to them, "Why do you seek the living among the dead? 6 He is not here, but has risen. Remember how he told you, while he was still in Galilee, 7 that the Son of Man must be delivered into the hands of sinful men and be crucified and on the third day rise." 8 And they remembered his words, 9 and returning from the tomb they told all these things to the eleven and to all the rest. 10 Now it was Mary Magdalene and Joanna and Mary the mother of James and the other women with them who told these things to the apostles, 11 but these words seemed to them an idle tale, and they did not believe them. 12 But Peter rose and ran to the tomb; stooping and looking in, he saw the linen cloths by themselves; and he went home marveling at what had happened. On the Road to Emmaus. 13 That very day two of them were going to a village named Emmaus, about seven miles from Jerusalem, 14 and they were talking with each other about all these things that had happened. 15 While they were talking and discussing together, Jesus himself drew near and went with them. 16 But their eyes were kept from recognizing him. 17 And he said to them, "What is this conversation that you are holding with each other as you walk?" And they stood still, looking sad. 18 Then one of them, named Cleopas, answered him, "Are you the only visitor to Jerusalem who does not know the things that have happened there in these days?" 19 And he said to them, "What things?" And they said to him, "Concerning Jesus of Nazareth, a man who was a prophet mighty in deed and word before God and all the people, 20 and how our chief priests and rulers delivered him up to be condemned to death, and crucified him. 21 But we had hoped that he was the one to redeem Israel. Yes, and besides all this, it is now the third day since these things happened. 22 Moreover, some women of our company amazed us. They were at the tomb early in the morning, 23 and when they did not find his body, they came back saying that they had even seen a vision of angels, who said that he was alive. 24 Some of those who were with us went to the tomb and found it just as the women had said, but him they did not see." 25 And he said to them, "O foolish ones, and slow of heart to believe all that the prophets have spoken! 26 Was it not necessary that the Christ should suffer these things and enter into his glory?" 27 And beginning with Moses and all the Prophets, he interpreted to them in all the Scriptures the things concerning himself. 28 So they drew near to the village to which they were going. He acted as if he were going farther, 29 but they urged him strongly, saying, "Stay with us, for it is toward evening and the day is now far spent." So he went in to stay with them. 30 When he was at table with them, he took the bread and blessed and broke it and gave it to them. 31 And their eyes were opened, and they recognized him. And he vanished from their sight. 32 They said to each other, "Did not our hearts burn within us while he talked to us on the road, while he opened to us the Scriptures?" 33 And they rose that same hour and returned to Jerusalem. And they found the eleven and those who were with them gathered together, 34 saying, "The Lord has risen indeed, and has appeared to Simon!" 35 Then they told what had happened on the road, and how he was known to them in the breaking of the bread.

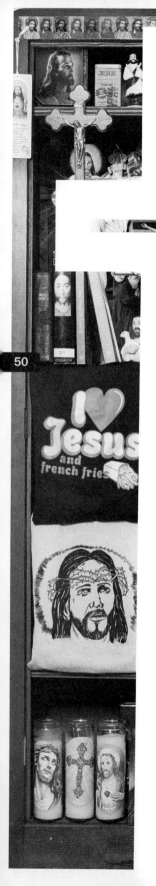

Luke 24:36 - 43

Jesus Appears to His Disciples 36 As they were talking about these things, Jesus himself stood among them, and said to them, "Peace to you!" 37 But they were startled and frightened and thought they saw a spirit. 38 And he said to them, "Why are you troubled, and why do doubts arise in your hearts? 39 See my hands and my feet, that it is I myself. Touch me, and see. For a spirit does not have flesh and bones as you see that I have." 40 And when he had said this, he showed them his hands and his feet. 41 And while they still disbelieved for joy and were marveling, he said to them, "Have you anything here to eat?" 42 They gave him a piece of broiled fish, 43 and he took it and ate before them.

1 Corinthians 15:3 - 9

For I delivered to you as of first importance what I also received: that Christ died for our sins in accordance with the Scriptures, 4 that he was buried, that he was raised on the third day in accordance with the Scriptures, 5 and that he appeared to Cephas, then to the twelve. 6 Then he appeared to more than five hundred brothers at one time, most of whom are still alive, though some have fallen asleep. 7 Then he appeared to James, then to all the apostles. 8 Last of all, as to one untimely born, he appeared also to me. 9 For I am the least of the apostles, unworthy to be called an apostle, because I persecuted the church of God.

John 20:24 - 29

Now Thomas, one of the Twelve, called the Twin, was not with them when Jesus came. 25 So the other disciples told him, "We have seen the Lord." But he said to them, "Unless I see in his hands the mark of the nails, and place my finger into the mark of the nails, and place my hand into his side, I will never believe." 26 Eight days later, his disciples were inside again, and Thomas was with them. Although the doors were locked, Jesus came and stood among them and said, "Peace be with you." 27 Then he said to Thomas, "Put your finger here, and see my hands; and put out your hand, and place it in my side. Do not disbelieve, but believe." 28 Thomas answered him, "My Lord and my God!" 29 Jesus said to him, "Have you believed because you have seen me? Blessed are those who have not seen and yet have believed."

NOTES

Evidence of Resurrection

1. dead
2. dead for our sin
3. died w/ sinners
4. without sin
5. returned after life
6. satisfied after return
7. prophecy 700 yrs. before Christ
   3 days he will raise

Luke 24 med doc - said Jesus was dead

no body in tomb
Luke 24:36 Peace be with you
            says Jesus

He was bodily alive - he wanted to eat.
(Ate a meal)
appeared 40 days after dead

1st Corinthians: 15 few years after
Paul he died resurrection
      buried
      raised on 3rd day
500 people at one time saw Jesus
after resurrection
James + Jude - brothers - after resurrection
they believed.
Thomas saw + believed

DISCUSSION QUESTIONS

1. Do you believe Jesus is alive right now?

_____

_____

_____

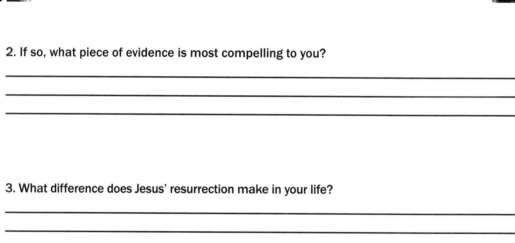

...there is no way to be a Christian and believe in the Jesus of the Bible unless you do believe that He did rise from death.

52

2. If so, what piece of evidence is most compelling to you?

_____

_____

_____

3. What difference does Jesus' resurrection make in your life?

_____

_____

_____

Jesus died, like the Scriptures foreshadowed. He was buried, just like they said He would be, and He rose three days later, just as was prophesied.

4. Why have so many throughout history objected to the historical, physical resurrection of Jesus?

_____

_____

_____

> *...the resurrection of Jesus is a historical fact. The evidence is overwhelming...attempts to explain it away or dismiss it are not coherent or tenable. And the simple, plain, factual truth is this: right now, Jesus is alive.*

5. Who in your life needs to be presented with the evidence of Jesus' resurrection?

_____

_____

53

KEY THOUGHT

Evidence for the resurrection of Jesus Christ from the dead overwhelmingly supports this most fundamental tenet of the Christian faith.

PRAYER REQUESTS

_____

_____

_____

_____

_____

NOTES

_____

_____

_____

_____

_____

NOTES

WHERE IS JESUS TODAY?

Acts 1:9

...as they were looking on, he was lifted up, and a cloud took him out of their sight.

The answer to this question hinges upon whether or not you believe Jesus rose from death. If He did not, then He is currently nothing more than a heap of rotted remains buried in some Middle Eastern cemetery plot. If this is the case, then the only thing that remains alive of Him today is His impeccable reputation as a good teacher and a nice, moral man. However, if Jesus did rise from the grave as a fully alive, fully functioning physical man, the question then must be addressed, where is He now?

The Bible clearly teaches that Jesus died, was buried, rose from death and ascended back into the glory of Heaven where He currently reigns with all glory, power and authority with the Father. However, this teaching is contested among many popular religious and cultic groups today. Some negate Jesus' physical resurrection, claiming that it was only His spirit that rose from the grave. Some say He currently reigns as a god of His own planet where He spends His days impregnating women in order to populate His sci-fi kingdom. Some even say that Jesus' spirit returned to earth in 1914 and decided to set-up shop in Pittsburgh, of all places. Clearly, not all religious groups, even those claiming to be Christian, agree on where Jesus is today.

Our picture of Jesus is often too narrow because we fail to truly appreciate His glorified and exalted state in Heaven. We often think of Him as an effeminate man who spent all of his time walking around in a dress, hugging children and having picnics on the hillside with his hippie friends talking about their feelings. And while Jesus was a loving, caring, compassionate and gentle man, He is also the embodiment of all power, all authority, all righteousness and all judgment. It is in this state that He currently sits at the right hand of the Father in Heaven, unveiled and full of glory. He acts as the mediator between God and man and upon His return He will judge the world in righteousness for sin.

In this session we will answer the question, "Where is Jesus today?" and discuss why it is critical for us to see Him in His glorified, exalted state in Heaven.

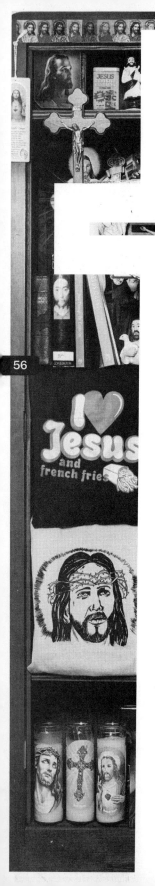

Acts 1:6 - 11

So when they had come together, they asked him, "Lord, will you at this time restore the kingdom to Israel?" 7 He said to them, "It is not for you to know times or seasons that the Father has fixed by his own authority. 8 But you will receive power when the Holy Spirit has come upon you, and you will be my witnesses in Jerusalem and in all Judea and Samaria, and to the end of the earth." 9 And when he had said these things, as they were looking on, he was lifted up, and a cloud took him out of their sight. 10 And while they were gazing into heaven as he went, behold, two men stood by them in white robes, 11 and said, "Men of Galilee, why do you stand looking into heaven? This Jesus, who was taken up from you into heaven, will come in the same way as you saw him go into heaven."

Isaiah 6:1 - 3

In the year that King Uzziah died I saw the Lord sitting upon a throne, high and lifted up; and the train of his robe filled the temple. 2 Above him stood the seraphim. Each had six wings: with two he covered his face, and with two he covered his feet, and with two he flew. 3 And one called to another and said: "Holy, holy, holy is the LORD of hosts; the whole earth is full of his glory!"

John 12:41

Isaiah said these things because he saw his glory and spoke of him.

Revelation 19:11 - 16

Then I saw heaven opened, and behold, a white horse! The one sitting on it is called Faithful and True, and in righteousness he judges and makes war. 12 His eyes are like a flame of fire, and on his head are many diadems, and he has a name written that no one knows but himself. 13 He is clothed in a robe dipped in blood, and the name by which he is called is The Word of God. 14 And the armies of heaven, arrayed in fine linen, white and pure, were following him on white horses. 15 From his mouth comes a sharp sword with which to strike down the nations, and he will rule them with a rod of iron. He will tread the winepress of the fury of the wrath of God the Almighty. 16 On his robe and on his thigh he has a name written, King of kings and Lord of lords.

Matthew 26:64

Jesus said to him, "You have said so. But I tell you, from now on you will see the Son of Man seated at the right hand of Power and coming on the clouds of heaven."

2 Corinthians 5:8

Yes, we are of good courage, and we would rather be away from the body and at home with the Lord.

John 14:2 - 3

In my Father's house are many rooms. If it were not so, would I have told you that I go to prepare a place for you? 3 And if I go and prepare a place for you, I will come again and will take you to myself, that where I am you may be also.

1 Timothy 2:5

For there is one God, and there is one mediator between God and men, the man Christ Jesus,

Hebrews 7:25

Consequently, he is able to save to the uttermost those who draw near to God through him, since he always lives to make intercession for them.

Matthew 28:16 - 20

Now the eleven disciples went to Galilee, to the mountain to which Jesus had directed them. 17 And when they saw him they worshiped him, but some doubted. 18 And Jesus came and said to them, "All authority in heaven and on earth has been given to me. 19 Go therefore and make disciples of all nations, baptizing them in the name of the Father and of the Son and of the Holy Spirit, 20 teaching them to observe all that I have commanded you. And behold, I am with you always, to the end of the age."

DISCUSSION QUESTIONS

1. Why is it important to see Jesus in His state of exaltation and not just His humble state of incarnation?

_____

_____

_____

58

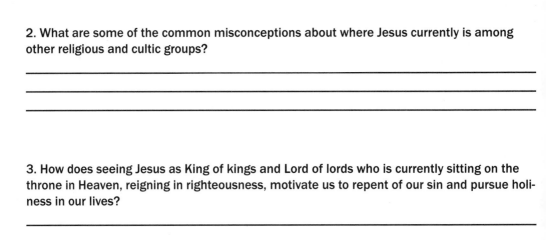

I don't know if the theme from The Jeffersons was playing, but moving on up, Jesus ascended back into heaven.

2. What are some of the common misconceptions about where Jesus currently is among other religious and cultic groups?

_____

_____

_____

3. How does seeing Jesus as King of kings and Lord of lords who is currently sitting on the throne in Heaven, reigning in righteousness, motivate us to repent of our sin and pursue holiness in our lives?

_____

_____

_____

...if we see Jesus as King of kings, Lord of lords, with a crown on His head, wearing white, seated upon His horse with a sword protruding from His mouth, coming with the angels to judge sinners and make war, it is to give us great incentive to repent of sin, be a friend of Jesus, not be a foe of Jesus, to change, not by being crushed, but by being repentant.

4. What responsibility did Jesus leave His followers upon His ascension into Heaven?

_____

_____

_____

> ...*almost everyone's portrait of Jesus is in His humble incarnation, not His glorious exaltation.*
>
> ...*the good news is that not only is Jesus alive and seated on a throne, but that as John reveals in Revelation 19, He will come back, there will be justice, and He will usher in a whole new kingdom.*

5. Who in your life needs to know that Jesus is exalted in Heaven, ruling with all authority?

_____

_____

_____

KEY THOUGHT

The teaching of the Bible is that Jesus died, was buried, rose three days later and shortly thereafter ascended back into the glory of Heaven where He had been in eternity past.

PRAYER REQUESTS

_____

_____

_____

_____

_____

NOTES

_____

_____

_____

_____

_____

NOTES

SESSION NINE

WHY SHOULD WE WORSHIP JESUS?

Romans 12:1

I appeal to you therefore, brothers, by the mercies of God, to present your bodies as a living sacrifice, holy and acceptable to God, which is your spiritual worship.

Worship is the setting up of someone or something in our lives as preeminent and of greatest importance. It is the assigning of value to someone or something and placing that person, object or idea in a position of glory, honor and esteem in our lives. Our worship is ultimately a reflection of what we treasure most. While it may be a car, a house, a hobby, a job, a salary, a dream or a spouse, the truth is that we all worship something or someone. And while the object of our worship may be unique, the truth remains the same for us all - we are all worshipers.

But worship is so much more than simply paying homage to something. It is living life assigning value to things and determining whether or not they are worthy of our sacrifice. It is deciding whether or not a particular person, thing or activity is worthy of our time, our energy, our money and our affections. Worship is choosing to sacrifice who we are in order to have, achieve or be a part of something else, something better.

The Bible teaches that Jesus is worthy of all worship and even records accounts of people coming to Him in order to worship Him as God. Still today, one of the distinguishing characteristics of Christianity is the worship of Jesus and the placing of Him in a position of glory in our lives. In doing so we not only claim that He is worthy of our praise, but that He is also worthy of our sacrifice to Him.

Our tendency, however, is to place more value on the things God has created (i.e. cars, jobs, sex, relationships, money, etc.) than on Him as the Creator. When what God has created is placed in a position of honor and esteem in our lives, above Him as the Creator, then we turn what was purposed for good into something very bad. It now holds a place in our hearts that it was never intended to hold. As a result, we sacrifice our lives for things that are not worthy of that honor and spend our lives on things that in the end do not deserve our worship.

In this session we will examine the truth that we are all worshipers at heart and discuss why Jesus is the only One worthy of our worship. We will also explore practically what it means to sacrificially offer our lives to Him as our ultimate act of love and devotion to Him.

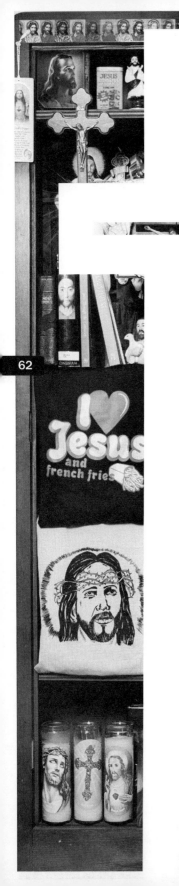

Romans 11:36 - 12:1
For from him and through him and to him are all things. To him be glory forever. Amen... 12:1 I appeal to you therefore, brothers, by the mercies of God, to present your bodies as a living sacrifice, holy and acceptable to God, which is your spiritual worship.

Romans 1:25
...they exchanged the truth about God for a lie and worshiped and served the creature rather than the Creator, who is blessed forever!

Exodus 20:1 - 5
And God spoke all these words, saying, 2 "I am the LORD your God, who brought you out of the land of Egypt, out of the house of slavery. 3 "You shall have no other gods before me. 4 "You shall not make for yourself a carved image, or any likeness of anything that is in heaven above, or that is in the earth beneath, or that is in the water under the earth. 5 You shall not bow down to them or serve them..."

NOTES

DISCUSSION QUESTIONS

1. How do you worship Jesus?

_____

_____

_____

> ...as Christians we do worship Jesus as God. And this means we don't just believe Jesus is God, but we respond to Him in ways that are obedient to Him as acts of worship.

2. Have you ever worshiped a "functional savior"? If so, who or what was it? What was the outcome?

_____

_____

_____

3. What person or thing in your life is the most likely candidate to become an idol?

_____

_____

_____

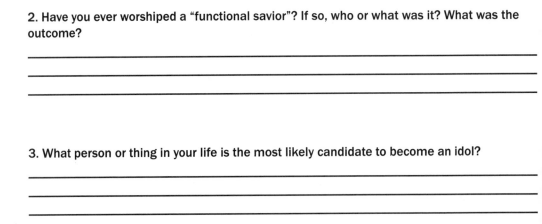

> What is worship? Some would say it's a musical style or it's an event that happens in a church building on a Sunday. The Bible has a more rich and broad definition of worship.
>
> Worship is living a life with a set of priorities that we make sacrifices for.

4. How is our worship of Jesus tied to our ultimate happiness?

_____

_____

_____

> *You may belong to Jesus by grace, but you're not worshiping Him unless He's in the position of glory, and the sacrifices that you're making are ultimately to glorify Him.*
>
> *...the question is not, will you worship? The question is, who or what will you worship?*

5. Who in your life needs to know about Jesus so that he or she can learn to worship Him?

_____

_____

_____

65

KEY THOUGHT

Everyone worships and has something or someone they are willing to make great sacrifices for.

PRAYER REQUESTS

_____

_____

_____

_____

NOTES

_____

_____

_____

_____

_____

NOTES

SESSION TEN

WHAT MAKES JESUS SUPERIOR TO OTHER SAVIORS?

Isaiah 43:11
I am the Lord, and besides me there is no savior.

A savior is someone or something that rescues us from a terrible plight or an uncomfortable predicament. Saviors are portrayed in all different forms through various media outlets in our culture. They are super heroes in movies who save the damsel in distress from the evil villain. They are commercials for lightweight, high-powered vacuum cleaners that save the overwhelmed mom from added stress and trouble. They are politicians clamoring for votes, claiming they will save the country from all its present peril. They are magazines in the checkout aisle giving sex tips that promise to save your sexually-starved relationship from becoming boring and predictable.

Whatever situation you might be struggling through in life or whatever pressures you may be facing, someone is sure to be selling a savior out there that promises to solve all your problems. The marketing strategy feeds off of the innate human desire to be saved by someone or something and promises that if you would just read that article, purchase that product, engage in that lifestyle or get involved in that relationship then your life will be more exciting, more passionate and ultimately more satisfying.

This innate human desire to be saved is not a bad thing, but it can never be satisfied outside of the person and work of Jesus. A healthy diet may keep us from becoming overweight, a boyfriend or girlfriend may keep us in a happy, committed relationship and a nice car may keep us from looking un-cool in the eyes of our friends. However, nothing but the grace of God can save us from the depths of sin in our soul and nobody but Jesus can rescue us from the consequences that sin has on our lives, both here in the present and for all eternity. He alone is the Messiah, the Savior who came to redeem us from our sin and save us from the wrath of God that was destined to fall upon us all. While the saviors this world has to offer may claim to revolutionize your life, none are able to save your life the way it needs to be saved. Only Jesus can do that, and only Jesus was willing to go to great lengths in order to accomplish that.

In this session we will define what a savior is, explore why Jesus is superior to other saviors and seek to identify some of the functional saviors we hold onto in our lives.

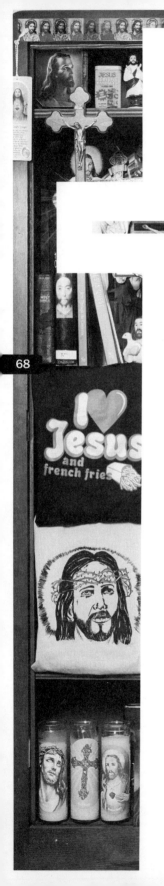

Luke 18:9 - 14

He also told this parable to some who trusted in themselves that they were righteous, and treated others with contempt: 10 "Two men went up into the temple to pray, one a Pharisee and the other a tax collector. 11 The Pharisee, standing by himself, prayed thus: 'God, I thank you that I am not like other men, extortioners, unjust, adulterers, or even like this tax collector. 12 I fast twice a week; I give tithes of all that I get.' 13 But the tax collector, standing far off, would not even lift up his eyes to heaven, but beat his breast, saying, 'God, be merciful to me, a sinner!' 14 I tell you, this man went down to his house justified, rather than the other. For everyone who exalts himself will be humbled, but the one who humbles himself will be exalted."

Isaiah 43:11

I am the LORD, and besides me there is no savior.

Isaiah 45:21

... there is no other god besides me, a righteous God and a Savior; there is none besides me.

Matthew 1:21

She will bear a son, and you shall call his name Jesus, for he will save his people from their sins.

Luke 2:11

For unto you is born this day in the city of David a Savior, who is Christ the Lord.

Titus 2:13

...waiting for our blessed hope, the appearing of the glory of our great God and Savior Jesus Christ...

Acts 4:12

And there is salvation in no one else, for there is no other name under heaven given among men by which we must be saved.

NOTES

DISCUSSION QUESTIONS

1. Is there anyone or anything in my life that I am trusting in as a functional savior?

_____

_____

_____

> *...whether it's Batman or Superman or Wolverine, there are saviors that are portrayed as a sort of mythical and fanciful means by which the world will be protected from tyranny and injustice and evil.*

2. In what ways do I need to return wholeheartedly to trusting in Jesus?

_____

_____

_____

3. What functional saviors do you see in the media?

_____

_____

_____

> *...deep within us there is this longing, this need, this passionate desire, to have someone be our savior.*

> *The difference between religion and Jesus is that in all religion, you are your savior and the religion exists to tell you how to save yourself. And in Christianity, Jesus is our Savior and He saves us.*

4. Why is it important to consider what your life would be like had Jesus not saved you?

_____

_____

_____

> *Religion can't save. Spirituality can't save. Morality can't save. A spouse can't save. A kid can't save. A boss can't save. A politician can't save. They may help you in some ways, but ultimately salvation is not their jurisdiction.*

5. Who do you know that is trusting in a functional savior and needs to be introduced to Jesus?

_____

_____

_____

KEY THOUGHT

The only true Savior is Jesus. He alone can save us from the grip of sin and the effects it has on our lives.

PRAYER REQUESTS

_____

_____

_____

_____

_____

NOTES

_____

_____

_____

_____

_____

_____

NOTES

SESSION ELEVEN
WHAT DIFFERENCE HAS JESUS MADE IN HISTORY?

Colossians 1:16-17
...all things were created through him and for him. 17 And he is before all things, and in him all things hold together.

No person in history has had as profound of an impact on the world we live in today as Jesus. All people of all races, ethnicities, sexual preference, political persuasion and religious conviction have in some way experienced the benefits of the person and work of Jesus in their lives. Every facet of the arts, politics, ethics, economics, law, human rights, science, and marriage and family values have been influenced, and in many cases, powerfully transformed by Jesus.

He spoke against the social tide of injustice towards women, children, the poor, the oppressed and the enslaved. He paved the way for a more biblical understanding of the value of all peoples and the dignity they deserve to be treated with. As a result, we have witnessed great social and legislative movements toward the equality of rights for men and women of all races. We have seen great value placed on the education of young people and significant measures taken to prevent them from being mistreated, abused and neglected.

The impact Jesus has had on ethics, justice and law is significant as well. It is illegal to murder, to steal, to cheat in business and to not pay your taxes. Thousands of non-profit and charitable organizations exist today for the sole purpose of meeting the needs of the poor and the oppressed in our world. And in the midst of a world governed by self-centeredness, individualism and a "survival of the fittest" philosophy for getting ahead, Jesus is the only explanation as to why governments, organizations and groups of individuals would fight for justice and mercy in this world, even at their own expense and sacrifice.

Jesus' impact throughout history has been clearly seen on a global scale, and the effects it has had on today are evident. But the question still remains, what impact has Jesus had on your life? How has His life transformed yours? Is He rewriting your history and setting a new course for your future?

In this session we will explore historically how Jesus' life has made a profound difference in history, and we will discuss practically how He can transform your life as well.

Matthew 19:14

Let the little children come to me and do not hinder them, for to such belongs the kingdom of heaven.

John 8:7

He who is without sin among you, let him be the first to throw a stone at her.

Exodus 20:15

You shall not steal.

Genesis 1:26

Let us make man in our image, after our likeness...

Matthew 7:21 - 23

"Not everyone who says to me, 'Lord, Lord,' will enter the kingdom of heaven, but the one who does the will of my Father who is in heaven. 22 On that day many will say to me, 'Lord, Lord, did we not prophesy in your name, and cast out demons in your name, and do many mighty works in your name?' 23 And then will I declare to them, 'I never knew you; depart from me, you workers of lawlessness.'

NOTES

DISCUSSION QUESTIONS

1. In what way has Jesus' life transformed different aspects of your life? (i.e. your vocation, education, family, etc.)

_____

_____

_____

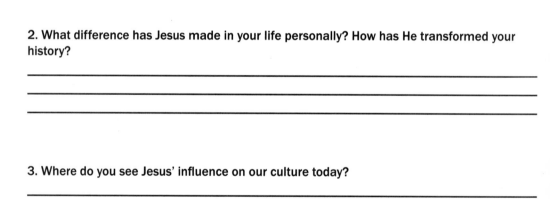

Jesus has absolutely transformed much of the world where His name has been made much of...

2. What difference has Jesus made in your life personally? How has He transformed your history?

_____

_____

_____

3. Where do you see Jesus' influence on our culture today?

_____

_____

_____

"I know men and I tell you that Jesus Christ is no mere man. Between Him and every other person in the world there is no possible term of comparison. Alexander, Caesar, Charlemagne, and I have founded empires, but on what did we rest the creation of our genius: upon force. Jesus Christ founded His empire upon love, and at this hour, millions of men would die for Him." ~ Napoleon

4. Why do you think some fail to recognize Jesus' impact on culture, while at the same time reaping the benefits of His influence?

_____

_____

_____

> Jesus is the most important, significant, influential person who has ever lived or will ever live in the history of the world.
>
> Jesus' teaching that everyone is equally an image bearer of God means that no human being is of any less dignity, value and worth as any other human being.

5. Who do you know that needs to have his or her life transformed by Jesus?

_____

_____

KEY THOUGHT

Jesus is the most important and influential person who has ever lived in the history of the world.

PRAYER REQUESTS

NOTES

NOTES

SESSION TWELVE

WHAT WILL JESUS DO UPON HIS RETURN?

2 Corinthians 5:10
For we must all appear before the judgment seat of Christ, so that each one may receive
what is due for what he has done in the body, whether good or evil.

Jesus is coming back. This truth is the certain hope that all followers of Jesus have in this life. In a world full of evil and injustice they can look to and long for with great expectancy the day He comes to righteously judge the world and put an end to all evil. To one day hear the words "well done good and faithful servant" from the lips of their Creator is the greatest motivation for Christians to live lives of holiness and obedience to Him today. The day Jesus comes back will be a day of great exultation for Christians as they stand before Him and receive the rewards that they will carry with them for all eternity in Heaven.

Yet while the return of Jesus will bring eternal blessings to all Christians, it will also bring eternal judgment to all non-Christians. The Bible is clear; everyone will stand before Jesus one day, Christians and non-Christians alike. Every knee will bow and every tongue will confess that Jesus is Lord. However, on that day some will bow to Him in great joy and some in great anguish.

The fate of all who do not place their faith in Jesus, love Him, adore Him, follow Him and submit their lives to His reign and rule is eternal condemnation and separation from God. The day Jesus comes back will be a day of great agony for non-Christians as they stand before Him and receive the condemnation they will carry with them for an eternity in Hell.

Some may accuse God of being cruel and unjust for allowing anyone to go to Hell. But for God not to punish the sins of man would be an act of injustice, thereby deeming Him unworthy to reign as the good and perfect Judge that He is. The great truth is that the goodness, mercy, love and justice of God are most clearly seen through the death of Jesus on the Cross. God, in His justice, satisfied the punishment for sin by laying it upon His Son, and in His goodness offered a way of salvation to us all. His justice and His goodness are not mutually exclusive, but are at all times working in perfect harmony.

In this session we will explore what Jesus will do upon His return for Christians and non-Christians alike, and evaluate the current state of our own relationships with Him.

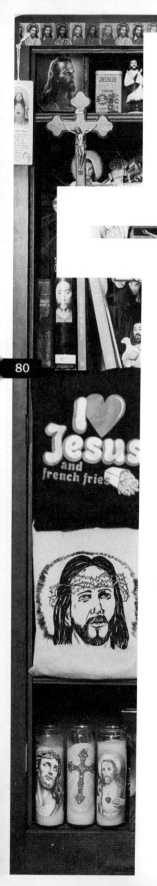

2 Peter 3:9

The Lord is not slow to fulfill his promise as some count slowness, but is patient toward you, not wishing that any should perish, but that all should reach repentance.

Romans 2:5

But because of your hard and impenitent heart you are storing up wrath for yourself on the day of wrath when God's righteous judgment will be revealed.

Daniel 12:2

And many of those who sleep in the dust of the earth shall awake, some to everlasting life, and some to shame and everlasting contempt.

Hebrews 9:27

And just as it is appointed for man to die once, and after that comes judgment...

2 Corinthians 5:8

Yes, we are of good courage, and we would rather be away from the body and at home with the Lord.

John 5:22

The Father judges no one, but has given all judgment to the Son...

Revelation 20:12 - 13

And I saw the dead, great and small, standing before the throne, and books were opened. Then another book was opened, which is the book of life. And the dead were judged by what was written in the books, according to what they had done. 13 And the sea gave up the dead who were in it, Death and Hades gave up the dead who were in them, and they were judged, each one of them, according to what they had done.

Revelation 14:10

...he also will drink the wine of God's wrath, poured full strength into the cup of his anger, and he will be tormented with fire and sulfur in the presence of the holy angels and in the presence of the Lamb.

Philippians 2:10 - 11

...at the name of Jesus every knee should bow, in heaven and on earth and under the earth, 11 and every tongue confess that Jesus Christ is Lord, to the glory of God the Father.

Ephesians 2:8-10

For by grace you have been saved through faith. And this is not your own doing; it is the gift of God, 9 not a result of works, so that no one may boast. 10 For we are his workmanship, created in Christ Jesus for good works, which God prepared beforehand, that we should walk in them.

2 Corinthians 5:9 - 10

So whether we are at home or away, we make it our aim to please him. 10 For we must all appear before the judgment seat of Christ, so that each one may receive what is due for what he has done in the body, whether good or evil.

Hebrews 12:1 - 3

...let us run with endurance the race that is set before us, 2 looking to Jesus, the founder and perfecter of our faith, who for the joy that was set before him endured the cross, despising the shame, and is seated at the right hand of the throne of God. 3 Consider him who endured from sinners such hostility against himself, so that you may not grow weary or fainthearted.

THE CHRISTOLOGY OF JESUS

DISCUSSION QUESTIONS

1. As a group, ask the questions of one another, "Am I a Christian?" How do you know?

_____

_____

_____

> *...the gap of time between Jesus' ascension back into heaven and whenever He should return is not a period of slowness, but a period of patience.*

> *...this life is one of two things for us all: a patient opportunity for salvation or an ongoing accumulation of reasons for damnation.*

2. Are you walking in the good works that He has prepared in advance for you to do? If not, what needs to change?

_____

_____

_____

3. What would you anticipate Jesus would say to you and how He might reward you if you were to die today?

_____

_____

_____

> *...you need to know this, nobody gets away with anything. There are people all over the world that think they are getting away with all kinds of sin, and they don't.*

4. How are you using this period of patience before the return of Christ to share Jesus with others who need to know Him?

_____

_____

_____

> *The question is not, will you be with Jesus forever? The question is, will it be as friend or foe?*
>
> *Just as there is justice in hell, there is justice in heaven. Just as the punishment fits the crime, so the reward fits the life.*

5. Who do you know that needs to know Jesus the way that you do?

_____

_____

_____

KEY THOUGHT

We will all stand before Christ one day and be judged for what we have done and for what we have failed to do in this life.

PRAYER REQUESTS

_____

_____

_____

_____

_____

NOTES

_____

_____

_____

_____

_____

NOTES

Additional Resources
available by

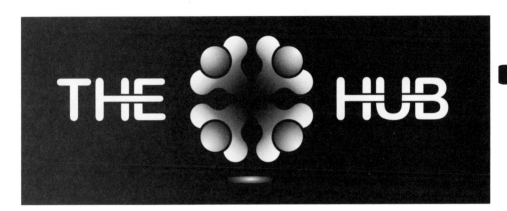

www.gotothehub.com

TRUTH DELIVERED

Study Guide
recommended
for each
participant.

NEW! Philippians
To Live is Christ & to Die is Gain
Video Teaching Series. Buy. Rent. Download.

The story begins in Philippi. Where Paul introduces three individuals that were all enslaved by the kind of things we often choose over the gospel.

• Lydia, the Business Executive
• The Little Slave Girl
• The Hard Working Jailer

Their lives portray dysfunction and emptiness but are totally transformed by the Gospel. True joy and Christ's love begin to live within them, giving them a life of purpose.

In fact, Paul himself was enslaved and then by God's grace and mercy he could pen these popular and profound words:

To live is Christ & to die is gain
I can do all things through Christ who strengthens me

Let's join Matt Chandler, Pastor of The Village Church in Dallas, Texas, as he walks us through Philippians. In this, one of the most intimate of Paul's letters, he paints a beautiful picture of what it is to be a mature Christian.

About

MATT CHANDLER serves as Lead Pastor of The Village Church in Highland Village, TX. He describes his tenure at The Village as a re-planting effort where he was involved in changing the theological and philosophical culture of the congregation. The church has witnessed a tremendous response growing from 160 people to over 8,000 including satellite campuses in Dallas and Denton. He is one of the most downloaded teachers on iTunes and consistently remains in the Top 5 of all national Religion and Spirituality Podcasts. Matt's passion is to speak to people in America and abroad about the glory of God and beauty of Jesus.

His greatest joy outside of Jesus is being married to Lauren and being a dad to their three children, Audrey, Reid and Norah.

TRUTH DELIVERED

NEW! Love Life
Song of Solomon
Video Teaching Series. Buy. Rent. Download.

What does it really mean to love? What does love look like in singleness, dating or marriage?

Through the study of Song of Solomon, Mark Driscoll reveals an Old Testament understanding of biblical sexuality with current cultural clarity.

Learn to celebrate God's gift of love in all of life by walking through this timely series.

87

About

PASTOR MARK DRISCOLL founded Mars Hill Church in Seattle in the fall of 1996. The church has grown from a small Bible study to over 10,000 people. He co-founded and is president of the Acts 29 Church Planting Network which has planted over 200 churches. He has authored The Radical Reformission, Death by Love, Religion Saves, Doctrine and many more.

Most of all, Mark and his high school sweetheart, Grace, enjoy raising their three sons and two daughters.

THE HUB

TRUTH DELIVERED

Study Guide recommended for each participant.

NEW! Ruth
A True Story of Love & Redemption
Video Teaching Series. Buy. Rent. Download.

Ruth is a courageous woman. Boaz is a generous man. Both exemplified great character. Ruth needed a redeemer. We all need a redeemer.

The Book of Ruth is simply put the greatest love story, ever. Tommy Nelson, Author, Pastor, and Teacher will lead us through this compelling story of Romance & Redemption.

In this journey you will learn:
- The Character of a Great Woman
- The Character of a Great Man
- How to Find God's Will for Life
- Your Redeemer
- Our King

Tommy Nelson

About

TOMMY NELSON has been the pastor of Denton Bible Church, in Denton, Texas, since 1977. Tommy graduated from the University of North Texas with a Bachelor's Degree in Education. He then attended Dallas Theological Seminary in Dallas, Texas, where he received the Master of Arts in Biblical Studies degree.

Tommy has been married to Teresa Nelson since 1974. They have two grown sons, Ben and John, along with five grandchildren.

Study Guide recommended for each participant.

Romans, Volume I & II
The Letter that Changed the World
Video Teaching Series. Buy. Rent. Download.

The most important idea in the Bible is how a Holy God can get a sinful man into Heaven and not compromise who He is. Romans tell us just that! It sits as Master of the House before all of Paul's writings. It is the Bible in miniature. It is the most important singular document ever penned by man and only inspiration could make it so.

In our study in Romans we will look at Paul's unfolding logic and incisive reasoning as to the divinity and holiness of the Christian gospel. When this book has been understood, reformation and new life follow shortly.

About

TOMMY NELSON has been the Pastor of Denton Bible Church, in Denton, Texas, since 1977. Tommy graduated from the University of North Texas with a Bachelor's Degree in Education. He then attended Dallas Theological Seminary in Dallas, Texas, where he received the Master of Arts in Biblical Studies degree.

Tommy has been married to Teresa since 1974. They have two grown sons, Ben and John, along with five grandchildren.

TRUTH DELIVERED

Study Guide recommended for each participant.

Song of Solomon 2005
Video Teaching Series. Buy. Rent. Download.

Used and loved throughout the world, the Song of Solomon series teaches the biblical design for relationships. For both singles and married couples, this study follows Solomon's relationship from attraction to dating and courtship, marriage and intimacy to resolving conflict, keeping romance alive and committing to the end. The 10th Anniversary Edition (released in 2005) updates Tommy Nelson's original study with updated teaching and added features.

Study Guide recommended for each participant.

SOS for Students
Video Teaching Series. Buy. Rent. Download.

Every parent, student pastor and student know the absolute need of saying, "an ounce of prevention is worth a pound of cure." God gave us the gift of love, marriage and sexuality, but since Christians have been mostly silent on this issue, many students learn these things from the secular community. As a result, students have a distorted view of sexuality and God's purpose for it.

Song of Solomon for Students teaches that God is for love and sexuality; in fact, it is His design and gift in the first place. Tommy Nelson taught these 6, 25 minute sessions to junior and senior high students. It will walk them through the first four chapters of Song of Solomon and focuses on these issues: attraction, dating and the truth about sexuality and when it is most enjoyed and most honoring to God.

R RE:LIT

Pastor Mark Driscoll founded Mars Hill Church in Seattle in the fall of 1996. The church has grown from a small Bible study to over 10,000 people. He co-founded and is president of the Acts 29 Church Planting Network which has planted over 200 churches. He has authored The Radical Reformission, Death by Love, Religion Saves, Doctrine and many more.

91

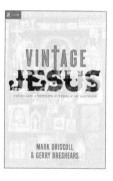

Vintage Jesus

Timeless Answers to
Timely Questions

This popular-level theology book introduces the person and work of Christ to those who are seeking answers to some of their most basic–and pivotal–questions.

Vintage Church

Timeless Truths and
Timely Methods

This popular-level theology book paints a portrait of the church that is timeless in all that it believes and timely in all that it does.

Excerpt on page 92.

Death by Love

Letters from the Cross

Real people. Real sin. Transformed lives. Deep theology meets gritty pastoral experiences as *Death by Love* explains the practical implications of what Jesus accomplished on the cross. This compilation of heartfelt letters written from a pastor to his people is for all those who have sinned and have been sinned against.

A Book You'll Actually Read series

On the New Testement
On the Old Testement
On Who Is God?
On Church Leadership

All-in-one concise books you'll actually read!

VIN†AGE CHURCH

TIMELESS TRUTHS *and* TIMELY METHODS

MARK DRISCOLL
& GERRY BRESHEARS

Chapter 2 – What Is a Christian Church?

And they devoted themselves to the apostles' teaching and the fellowship, to the breaking of bread and the prayers. And awe came upon every soul, and many wonders and signs were being done. — Acts 2:42–43

A few billion people worship Jesus Christ as God every week and do so in the church as the church. Yet, if you walk into various churches and ask the people who comprise that church what the word *church* means, the odds are that you will get either a blank stare or a series of conflicting definitions.

Sadly, this is even true from their pastors. In preparing for this book I asked various pastors of some of America's largest churches—godly men and dear friends—if they have a working definition of the church. And not one of them did; they confessed they were giving their lives to building something of which they did not even have a clear definition.

Their response was not surprising because for much of the history of the church the definition of the church has simply been assumed. For example, the Nicene Creed says, "we believe in one holy catholic and apostolic church." Yet, it does not define what is meant by "the church," but rather assumes that we already know.

The assumption that Christians innately know what the church is has a long history. The early church debated many things such as the Trinity and the relationship between the humanity and divinity of Jesus Christ. However, one issue it did not debate was what constitutes the church. After Cyprian, Bishop of Carthage, wrote *The Unity of the Church* in 251A.D. until Wycliffe wrote *The Church* in 1378, there was no significant monograph on the church.[1]

Everything changed in the sixteenth century when the Reformation forced Protestants and Roman Catholics alike to actually define church. This led to numerous definitions and debates, which continue to this day with no widespread agreement. For example, the *Evangelical Dictionary of Theology* says

> The Arnoldists emphasized poverty and identification with the masses; the Waldenses stressed literal obedience to Jesus' teachings and emphasized evangelical preaching. Roman Catholics claimed that the only true church was that over which the pope was supreme as successor of the apostle Peter. The Reformers Martin Luther and John Calvin, following John Wycliffe, distinguished between the visible and invisible church, claiming that the invisible church consists of the elect only. Thus an individual, including the pope, might be a part of the visible church but not a part of the invisible and true church."[2]

Part of the confusion is that the Greek word *ekklesia*, which is translated "church," has a wide range of meaning.[3] Originally, it sometimes designated any public assembly, including a full-blown riot.[4] In the Septuagint (the Greek translation of the Hebrew Old Testament), the word is translated *qahal*, which designates the assembly of God's people.[5] So in the New Testament *ekklesia* may signify the assembly of the Israelites.[6] Most of the uses of the word *ekklesia* in the New Testament designate the Christian church, both the local church[7] and the universal church.[8]

The English word "church" derives from the Greek word *kyriakon*, which means "the Lord's."[9] Later it came to mean the Lord's house, a church building. This increases the confusion because nowhere in the New Testament does church in any of its forms refer to a building. Wayne Grudem helpfully summarizes the uses of "church":

A "house church" is called a "church" in Romans 16:5 ("greet also *the church in their house*"), 1 Corinthians 16:19 ("Aquila and Prisca, together with *the church in their house*, send you hearty greetings in the Lord"). The church in an entire city is also called "a church" (1 Cor. 1:2; 2 Cor. 1:1; and 1 Thess. 1:1). The church in a region is referred to as a "church" in Acts 9:31: "So *the church throughout all Judea and Galilee and Samaria* had peace and was built up." Finally, the church throughout the entire world can be referred to as "the church." Paul says, "Christ loved *the church* and gave himself up for her" (Eph. 5:25) and says, "God has appointed *in the church* first apostles, second prophets, third teachers . . ." (1 Cor. 12:28). . . . We may conclude that the group of God's people considered at any level from local to universal may rightly be called "a church."[10]

Various Christian traditions are prone to define the church—or their church—in an unhealthy and reductionistic manner, focusing on one primary metaphor at the expense of the full breadth of New Testament teaching. As a result, they become imbalanced in some way and therefore unhealthy. For example, the corporate church is referred to as the bride of Christ. The result of overemphasizing this metaphor is the effeminate nature of much of evangelical preaching and singing.[11]

We must devote this chapter to defining the *being* of the church before we turn to the *well being* of the church in the rest of the book. The definition of what constitutes a Christian church is vitally important, especially in our day when cultists and oddball, self-appointed spiritual gurus keep starting various kinds of pseudo-churches. The church is also a hot issue among younger pastors today. In previous generations singles' ministry, student ministry, and parachurch ministry were the hot options for entrepreneurial young leaders. But today the hot ministry is church planting in every form. This includes churches within churches seeking to reach people outside the existing church, house churches, multi-campus churches, and traditional church planting. This phenomenon is spreading across all denominational and theological traditions with no clear understanding of exactly what a church is or does.

Furthermore, the effort to cultivate the most innovative and effective postmodern church has led to a market of books that nearly always start with some word followed by "church," such as *Liquid Church, Emerging Church, Organic Church, Missional Church, Multi-Site Church, Externally Focused Church, House Church, Future Church, Ancient-Future Church, Blogging Church,* and *Prevailing Church*. What is curious about most of the books on the church is that very rarely do any of them actually define what the church is, or even clarify what the church does. Instead, most of the books simply share best practices gleaned from "successful" churches. This is curious because without a definition of what a church is or does, I'm unsure how we can even deem one successful. Therefore, we will establish a definition of the local church:

The local church is a community of regenerated believers who confess Jesus Christ as Lord. In obedience to Scripture they organize under qualified leadership, gather regularly for preaching and worship, observe the biblical sacraments of baptism and communion, are unified by the Spirit, are disciplined for holiness, and scatter to fulfill the great commandment and the great commission as missionaries to the world for God's glory and their joy.

This definition is summarized from Acts 2. As we study through that text, we will see eight characteristics of the true local church, which is an incarnation of the universal church. I believe understanding these characteristics will be helpful to many churches and their leaders, thanks to Gerry's helpful insights gleaned over many decades of study on this issue. A true church is one characterized by:

1. Regenerated church membership
2. Qualified leadership
3. Preaching and worship
4. Rightly administered sacraments
5. Spirit unity
6. Holiness
7. The great commandment to love
8. The great commission to evangelize and make disciples

1. T. F. Torrance, *Theology in Reconstruction* (Grand Rapids, MI: Wm. B. Eerdmans Publishing Co., 1965), 266.

2. R. L. Omanson, "The Church," in *Evangelical Dictionary of Theology*, ed. Walter A. Elwell (Grand Rapids, MI: Baker Books, 1984), 231.

3. See R. L. Omanson, "The Church," in *Evangelical Dictionary of Theology*, ed. Walter A. Elwell (Grand Rapids, MI: Baker Books, 1984), 231.

4. Acts 19:32, 39, 41.

5. Deut. 10:4; 23:2–3; 31:30; Ps. 22:23.

6. Acts 7:38; Heb. 2:12.

7. Matt. 18:17; Acts 15:41; Rom. 16:16; 1 Cor. 4:17; 7:17; 14:33; Col. 4:15.

8. Matt. 16:18; Acts 20:28; 1 Cor. 12:28; 15:9; Eph. 1:22.

9. 1 Cor. 11:20; Rev. 1:10.

10. Wayne Grudem, *Systematic Theology: An Introduction to Biblical Doctrine* (Grand Rapids, MI: Zondervan, 1994), 857.

11. This is what David Murrow speaks of in his book, *Why Men Hate Going to Church* (Nashville: Thomas Nelson, 2004).

NOTES